J676

FIND OUT ABOUT

Paper

© 1994 Watts Books

Watts Books
96 Leonard Street
London EC2A 4RH

Franklin Watts Australia
14 Mars Road
Lane Cove
NSW 2066

UK ISBN· 0 7496 1627 X

10 9 8 7 6 5 4 3 2 1

Dewey Decimal Classification 676

A CIP catalogue record for this book
is available from the British Library

Editor: Annabel Martin
Design: Thumb Design

Photographs: S. & M. Biddle 21; Chris Fairclough
Colour Library 4, 12, 13, 15, 17, 18, 19, 20, 25, 26, 27;
Ecoscene © Sally Morgan 6, © Cooper 30;
Eye Ubiquitous © Yiorgos Nikiteas 29 (inset);
Robert Harding Picture Library 5, 11, 16, 22, 24, 31,
© Paolo Koch 28; ZEFA 9, 14, 29 (main);
By kind permission of the Board of Trustees
of the Victoria & Albert Museum 23.

Printed in Hong Kong

FIND OUT ABOUT

Henry Pluckrose

Watts Books

London • New York • Sydney

These tall trees are being cut down.

They will be taken
to a paper mill
to be turned into paper.

At the mill the trunks are cut into tiny pieces.

These are crushed
and soaked in water.
Machines beat the wood
and water together
to make a mixture.
This mixture is called pulp.
Chemicals are added
to the pulp.
They make the paper
smooth to write on.

The water is then drained from the wet paper pulp.

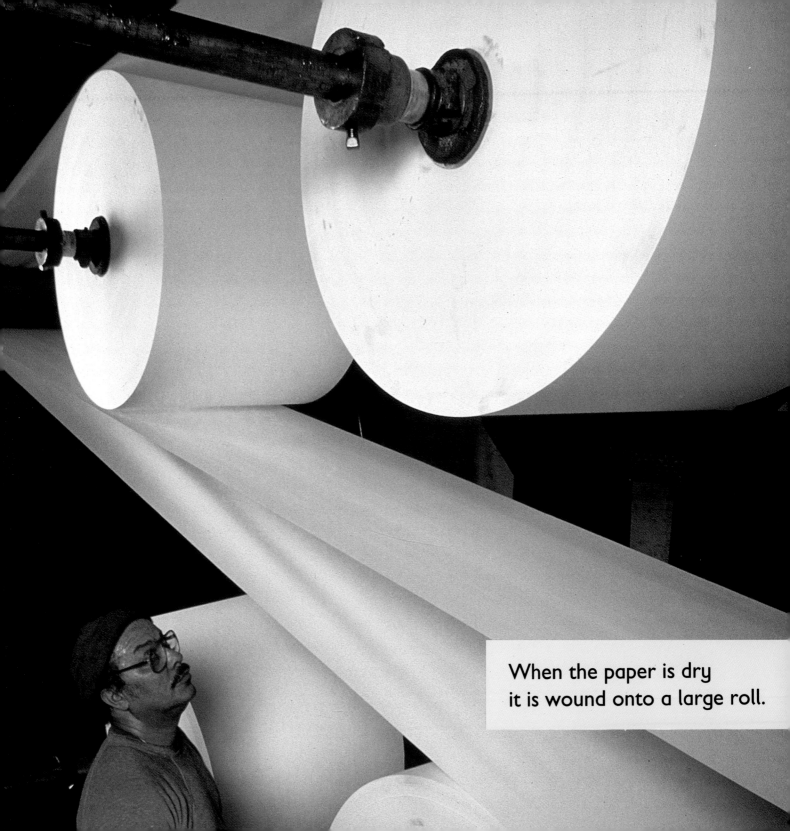

When the paper is dry
it is wound onto a large roll.

We use paper
in many different ways.
Books are made of paper
onto which words and pictures
have been printed . . .

and so are newspapers
and magazines.

We write letters
on paper . . .

and paper is used
to print out information
which has been stored
on computer.

Paper is made
in many different thicknesses.
The paper used to make
these delicate lanterns
is very light and thin.

Much heavier paper
is used to package food.
Very heavy paper
is called card.

Paper can be used
in large sheets . . .

or in very tiny pieces.

Postage stamps are printed on large sheets of paper too. Tiny holes along their edges make it easy to tear each stamp from the sheet on which it is printed.

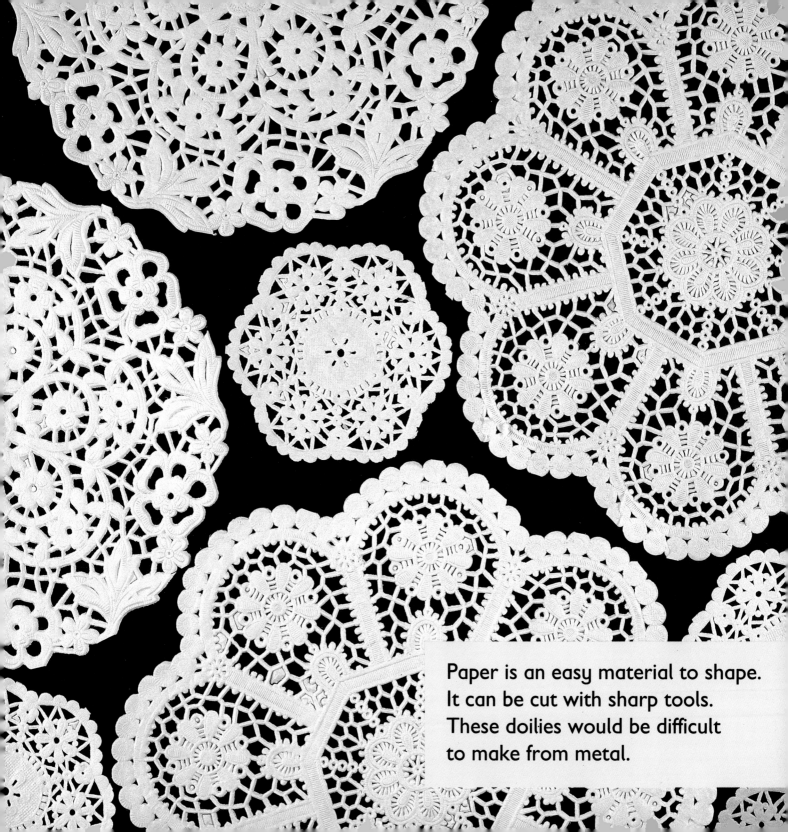

Paper is an easy material to shape.
It can be cut with sharp tools.
These doilies would be difficult
to make from metal.

It is easy to join
one piece of paper to another –
with glue, staples, clips or pins.

Papers of all kinds
are used by artists.
Three hundred years ago
Japanese artists
invented ways of folding paper
to make pictures and models.
The art of paper-folding
is called Origami.

In China, kites made of paper are flown on holidays and festivals. Why is paper a good material to use to make a kite?

Paper is also used to make
pictures and window hangings.
A shape cut from
one piece of paper
is called a silhouette.

Paper is often coloured and decorated.
We use decorated paper
on the walls of our homes . . .

and to wrap presents.

Not all paper feels the same
to the touch.
Paper can be very soft and absorbent.
Kitchen towels have to be able
to soak up liquids.
Rough toilet paper would be
very unpleasant to use!

Paper and card used
to pack heavy goods
has to be strong and tough.

To make paper strong, scraps of cotton and cloth are mixed into the pulp. Bank notes are made of very hard-wearing paper.

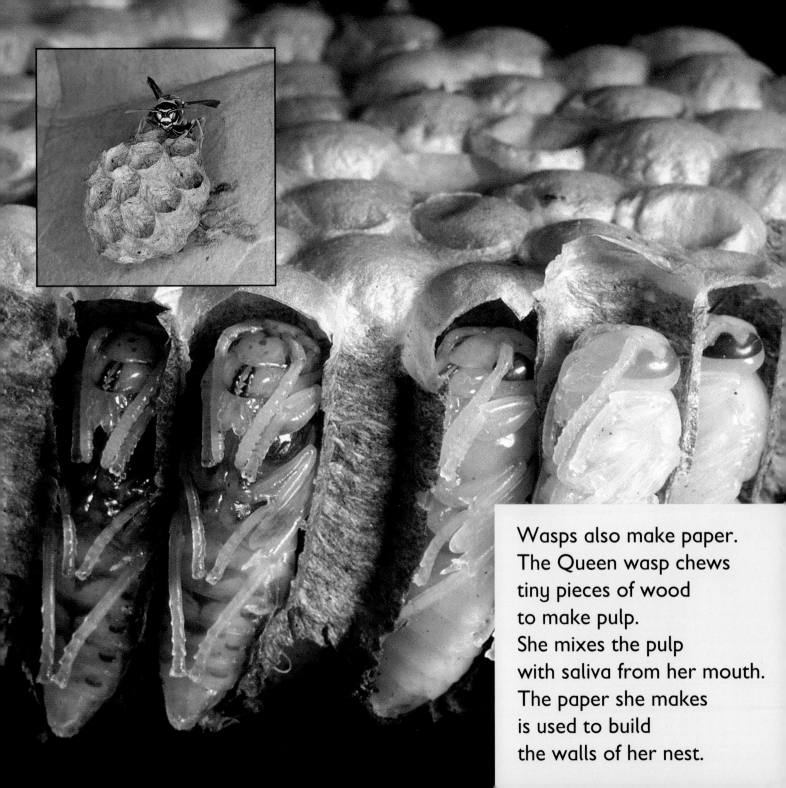

Wasps also make paper.
The Queen wasp chews
tiny pieces of wood
to make pulp.
She mixes the pulp
with saliva from her mouth.
The paper she makes
is used to build
the walls of her nest.

PAPER
BANK

Old paper can be re-used.
If it is returned to the paper mill,
old paper can be cleaned
and used to make new pulp.

Using old material again
is called re-cycling.
By pulping used paper
we can save the world's forests.
Can you think how?

About this book

This book is designed for use in the home, kindergarten and infant school.

Parents can share the book with young children. Its aim is to bring into focus some of the elements of life and living which are all too often taken for granted. To develop fully, all young children need to have their understanding of the world deepened and the language they use to express their ideas extended. This book, and others in the series, takes the everyday things of the child's world and explores them, harnessing curiosity and wonder in a purposeful way.

For those working with young children each book is designed to be used both as a picture book, which explores ideas and concepts and as a starting point to talk and exploration. The pictures have been selected because they are of interest in themselves and also because they include elements which will promote enquiry. Talk can lead to displays of items and pictures collected by children and teacher. Pictures and collages can be made by the children themselves.

Everything in our environment is of interest to the growing child. The purpose of these books is to extend and develop that interest.

Henry Pluckrose